Peter I. Tschaikowsky / Tchaikovsky

(1840–1893)

Der Nussknacker

Ballett in zwei Akten, op. 71

Für Klavier leicht bearbeitet von
Hans-Günter Heumann

Handlung erzählt von Monika Heumann
Zeichnungen von Brigitte Smith

The Nutcracker

A ballet in two acts, Op. 71

In a simple arrangement for piano by
Hans-Günter Heumann

The story told by Monika Heumann
English version by Julia Rushworth

Drawings by Brigitte Smith

ED 23569
ISMN 979-0-001-21571-8
ISBN 978-3-7957-2572-3

SCHOTT

Mainz · London · Madrid · Paris · New York · Tokyo · Beijing
© 1998/2022 Schott Music GmbH & Co. KG, Mainz · Printed in Germany
www.schott-music.com

Liebe Klavierspielerin, lieber Klavierspieler,

in diesem Band wird eines der bezauberndsten und beliebtesten Ballette, *Der Nussknacker* (op. 71) von Peter Iljitsch Tschaikowsky (1840-1893), in leichter Bearbeitung für Klavier vorgestellt.

Neben dem *Nussknacker* schrieb Tschaikowsky auch die Musik zu *Schwanensee* und *Dornröschen*, zwei weiteren Marksteinen in der Geschichte des Balletts.

Tschaikowsky, der eine Aufführung der Erzählung E. T. A. Hoffmanns vom *Nussknacker und Mäusekönig* (umgearbeitet von Modest Tschaikowsky zu einem Kinderzimmerspiel) im Familienkreis miterlebt hatte, berichtete davon dem Choreographen Petipa. So entstand der Plan, aus dieser Nussknacker-Geschichte ein Ballett zu machen. Durch die Erkrankung Petipas übernahm sein Assistent Lew Iwanow die Realisierung des Projekts im Sinne Petipas, und dieser gab dem Komponisten besonders im 2. Akt einige Anregungen. Tschaikowsky beendete die Partitur im Sommer 1891.

In der Weihnachtszeit 1892 fand die Uraufführung des Balletts in St. Petersburg statt. *Der Nussknacker* gilt heute als Standardwerk, das sich in der Vorweihnachtszeit großer Beliebtheit erfreut. Es zeigt sich aber auch, dass kaum ein anderes Ballett des klassischen Repertoires heute so vielen Änderungen gegenüber der ursprünglichen Fassung unterworfen ist.

Aber nun tretet ein in die zauberhafte Märchenwelt des *Nussknackers* und erlebt die Abenteuer im musikalischen Sinne nach.

Euer
Hans-Günter Heumann

Dear Pianists,

In this volume you will find a simple arrangement for piano of one of the most enchanting and most popular ballets ever written: *The Nutcracker* (Op. 71) by Peter Ilyich Tchaikovsky (1840-1893).

As well as *The Nutcracker*, Tchaikovsky also wrote the music to *Swan Lake* and *The Sleeping Beauty*, two other landmarks in the history of ballet.

Having seen a family performance of E. T. A. Hoffmann's tale of *The Nutcracker and the Mouse King*, adapted by the composer's younger brother Modest Tchaikovsky into a play for children, Tchaikovsky described the play to the choreographer Petipa. Together they worked on a plan for a ballet based on the Nutcracker story. When Petipa fell ill, his assistant Lev Ivanov stepped in to work on the project as begun by Petipa; Ivanov made a few suggestions of his own which were taken up by the composer, in Act II in particular. Tchaikovsky completed the score in the summer of 1891.

In the Christmas period of 1892 the first performance of the ballet was given in St Petersburg. Nowadays *The Nutcracker* is part of the standard repertoire, and is always extremely popular in the time before Christmas. The original version has been reworked and adapted, however, more times than most other ballets in the classical repertoire.

And now step inside the magical fairytale world of the *Nutcracker* and enjoy the adventure as you follow the music.

With best wishes,
Hans-Günter Heumann

Inhalt

Steckbrief: Der Nussknacker 3
Steckbrief: Peter Iljitsch Tschaikowsky 4
Handlung 5
Ouvertüre 8
Begrüßung der Gäste 10
Marsch 11
Onkel Drosselmeyer 12
Klara und der Nussknacker 13
Großvatertanz 16
Pas de deux von Klara und dem
   Nussknacker-Prinzen 18
Schneeflocken-Walzer 20
Divertissement:
   Spanischer Tanz 22
   Arabischer Tanz 23
   Chinesischer Tanz 24
   Russischer Tanz (Trepak) 26
   Tanz der Rohrflöten 27
Mutter Gigogne 28
Blumenwalzer 30
Finale (Walzer) 34

Contents

History of the Work: The Nutcracker 3
Biography: Peter Ilyich Tchaikovsky 4
The Plot 5
Overture 8
Welcoming the Guests 10
March 11
Uncle Drosselmeyer 12
Clara and the Nutcracker 13
Grandfather's Dance 16
Pas de deux for Clara and the Nutcracker
   Prince 18
Snowflake Waltz 20
Divertissement:
   Spanish Dance 22
   Arabian Dance 23
   Chinese Dance 24
   Russian Dance (Trepak) 26
   Dance of the Reed Pipes 27
   Mother Gigogne 28
Waltz of the Flowers 30
Finale – Waltz 34

Steckbrief
Der Nussknacker

Uraufführung Dezember 1892 im Marynsky-Theater in St. Petersburg

Libretto Marius Petipa, nach E. T. A. Hoffmanns Märchen „Nussknacker und Mäusekönig"

Choreographie Lew Iwanow

Nussknacker-Suite op. 71a ist die Konzertfassung des gleichnamigen Balletts, mit insgesamt acht Stücken; uraufgeführt am 7. März 1892, mit Begeisterung des Publikums aufgenommen

History of the Work
The Nutcracker

First performed at the Marinsky theatre in St Petersburg in December 1892

Libretto by Marius Petipa, based on E.T.A. Hoffmann's fairy tale 'The Nutcracker and the Mouse King'

Choreography by Lev Ivanov

The Nutcracker Suite, Op. 71a, is the concert version of the ballet of the same name, consisting of eight pieces; it was first performed on 7 March 1892 and met with an enthusiastic response from the audience

Steckbrief
Peter I. Tschaikowsky

1840 geboren am 7. Mai in Wotkinsk (Russland)

1850 Eintritt in die Rechtsschule in St. Petersburg

1855–1858 Klavierunterricht ohne gründliche musikalische Unterweisung

1859 Beamter im Justizministerium

1863 Anregung zur Beschäftigung mit der Musik durch einen Freund. Beendigung des Staatsdienstes und Besuch des St. Petersburger Konservatoriums (Kompositionsunterricht bei A. Rubinstein)

1866–1877 Theorielehrer am Moskauer Konservatorium

1869–1875 Kompositionsreihe von Werken mit eigener Stilprägung, erste größere Erfolge

bis 1876 Musikkritiker bei den „Russischen Nachrichten"

1877 Heirat mit einer Konservatoriums-Schülerin. Trennung nach wenigen Wochen

1878 wurde Nadeschda F. von Meck seine Mäzenin.
Durch Erhalt von 6000 Rubel jährlich hatte er fortan keine finanziellen Sorgen mehr

ab 1878 lebte Tschaikowsky häufig im Ausland und widmete sich ausschließlich seinem kompositori-schen Schaffen

seit 1880 internationale Anerkennung seiner Werke und Auftreten als Dirigent

1893 Ehrendoktorwürde der Universität in Cambridge. Stirbt am 6. November in St. Petersburg

Biography
Peter I. Tchaikovsky

1840 born in Wotkinsk (Russia) on 7 May

1850 started at the school of Jurisprudence in St Petersburg

1855–1858 had piano lessons, but without any grounding in general musical principles

1859 entered the civil service at the ministry of Justice

1863 a friend stimulated his interest in music. He left the civil service and enrolled at the Conservatoire in St Petersburg (studying composition with A. Rubinstein)

1866–1877 taught music theory at the Moscow Conservatoire

1869–1875 composed a series of works with a recognizable individual style; enjoyed his first major musical successes

until 1876 music critic for the 'Russian News' paper

1877 married a music student; they separated after only a few weeks

1878 Nadeschda F. von Meck became Tchaikovsky's patroness. With the settlement of an annuity of 6000 roubles a year he was freed from any further financial worries

from 1878 Tchaikovsky spent much of his time living abroad, devoting all his energies to his work as a composer

from 1880 his compositions and performances as a conductor achieved international recognition

1893 received an honorary doctorate from the University of Cambridge. Tchaikovsky died in St Petersburg on 6 November

Handlung

1. Akt Im festlich geschmückten Weihnachtszimmer begrüßen der Präsident Silbermann und seine Frau die Gäste, die den Heiligen Abend mit ihnen und den Kindern verbringen sollen (**Begrüßung der Gäste**). Als die Uhr neun schlägt, tanzen die Kinder Klara und Franz mit ihren Cousins und Cousinen, Freunden und Freundinnen in das Weihnachtszimmer herein (**Marsch**) und bestaunen den prächtig geschmückten Weihnachtsbaum. Nun betritt plötzlich ein finster dreinblickender Mann den Raum, und die Kinder klammern sich erschrocken an ihre Eltern. Doch als der Vater ihn als **Onkel Drosselmeyer** vorstellt, sind alle gleich wieder fröhlich und staunen über die Geschenke, die dieser mitgebracht hat: vier mechanische Puppen, die tanzen können. Am meisten freut sich Klara über einen Nussknacker, den ihr Onkel Drosselmeyer schenkt. Franz will ihn auch haben und macht ihn beim Streit mit Klara kaputt (**Klara und der Nussknacker**).

The Plot

Act 1 In a drawing room adorned with Christmas decorations, Councillor Silbermann and his wife are greeting the guests who are to spend Christmas eve with them and their children (**Welcoming the Guests**). When the clock strikes nine, the children Clara and Franz come dancing into the room with their young cousins and friends (**March**) and gaze in admiration at the Christmas tree with its splendid decorations. All of a sudden, a man with a dark and mysterious look comes into the room and the children cling to their parents in fright. When their father introduces him as Uncle Drosselmeyer, however, they are all smiles again at once and marvel at the presents he has brought with him: four mechanical dancing dolls. Clara is happiest of all with a nutcracker that Uncle Drosselmeyer gives her. Franz wants to have him, too, and fights Clara over him, breaking the nutcracker (**Clara and the Nutcracker**).

Die Erwachsenen stellen sich zu einem letzten Tanz (**Großvatertanz**) auf und beenden damit den Abend. Als alle Gäste gegangen sind und das Weihnachtszimmer dunkel ist, kommt Klara im Nachthemd herein, um nach ihrem Nussknacker zu sehen. Die Uhr schlägt Mitternacht, und ein unheimliches Licht erhellt das Zimmer.

Der Weihnachtsbaum scheint zu wachsen, von allen Seiten kommen Mäuse, und der Nussknacker

The grown-ups get up for one last dance (**Grandfather's Dance**) to round off the evening. When all the guests have gone and the scene of the Christmas celebrations is in darkness, Clara comes down in her nightdress to look for her nutcracker. The clock strikes midnight and a mysterious light fills the room.

The Christmas tree seems to grow larger; mice appear from every corner, and the nutcracker comes

sowie alles übrige Spielzeug werden lebendig. Der Nussknacker kämpft an der Spitze von Pfefferkuchen-Soldaten gegen die Horde von Mäusen mit dem Mäusekönig als Anführer.

Nur durch Klaras Eingreifen siegt der Nussknacker und verwandelt sich in einen schönen Prinzen (**Pas de deux von Klara und dem Nussknacker-Prinzen**), der sie zum Dank in das Königreich der Zuckerfee mitnimmt.

Sie kommen durch einen Winterwald und sehen dem **Walzer der Schneeflocken** zu.

2. Akt Im Zuckerschloss berichtet der Nussknacker-Prinz dem ganzen Hofstaat, wie mutig Klara war. Ihr zu Ehren lässt die Zuckerfee ein herrlich gedecktes Tischlein bringen mit den Reichtümern des Königreichs der Süßigkeiten. Es werden Tänze gezeigt, die den Genüssen auf dem Tischlein zugeordnet sind. Zur Schokolade gehört der **spanische Tanz**, zum Kaffee der **arabische Tanz**, zum Tee der **chinesische Tanz**.

Daran schließt sich ein Kosakentanz (**russischer Tanz – Trepak**) an; als nächste treten die Rohrflöten auf (**Tanz der Rohrflöten**).

Mutter Gigogne tanzt in einem breiten Reifrock, unter dem kleine Harlekins hervorkommen. Es folgt ein großer **Blumenwalzer**. Nach weiteren Tänzen endet der Besuch bei der Zuckerfee mit einem **Walzer**, und Klara findet sich anschließend mit dem hölzernen Nussknacker im Weihnachtszimmer wieder.

to life, along with all the other toys. The nutcracker leads an army of gingerbread soldiers against the horde of mice with the mouse king as their leader. Only thanks to Clara's intervention does the nutcracker win the battle, and then he turns into a handsome prince (**Pas de deux for Clara and the Nutcracker Prince**) who shows his gratitude by taking her off with him to the kingdom of the Sugar Plum Fairy.

They pass through a wintry forest and watch the **Snowflake Waltz**.

Act 2 Inside the sugar castle the Nutcracker Prince tells all the courtiers how brave Clara has been. In her honour the Sugar Plum Fairy has a little table brought in laden with the most wonderful delights of the Kingdom of Sweets. Dances are performed to accompany the sweetmeats on the table. To go with the chocolate there is the **Spanish Dance**, with the coffee the **Arabian Dance**, and with the tea comes the **Chinese Dance**.

Then there is a Cossack dance (**Russian Dance – Trepak**), followed by the appearance of the reed pipes (**Dance of the Reed Pipes**).

Mother Gigogne dances in a wide hooped skirt, from under which little harlequins appear. Then there is a great **Waltz of the Flowers**. After more dancing the visit of the Sugar Plum Fairy ends with a **Waltz**, and Clara finds herself back in the drawing room with the Christmas tree with the wooden nutcracker.

Ouvertüre
Overture

Allegro giusto ♩ = 160 - 176

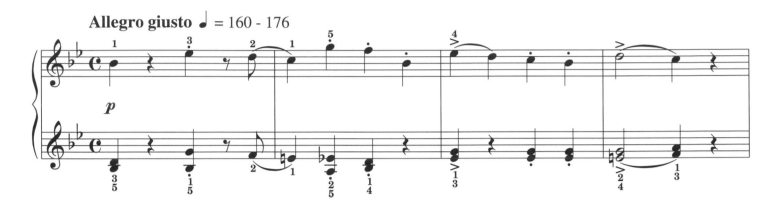

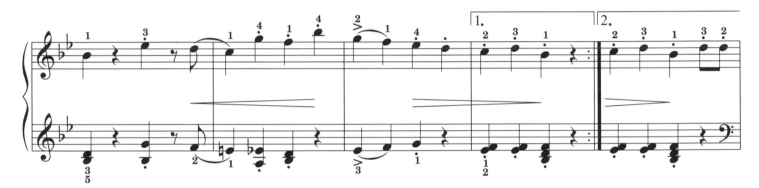

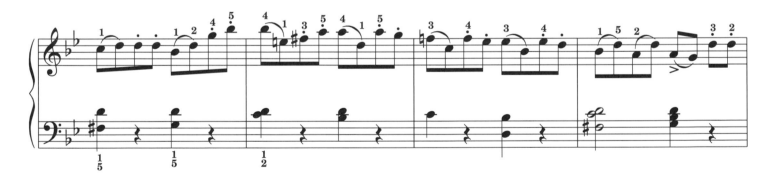

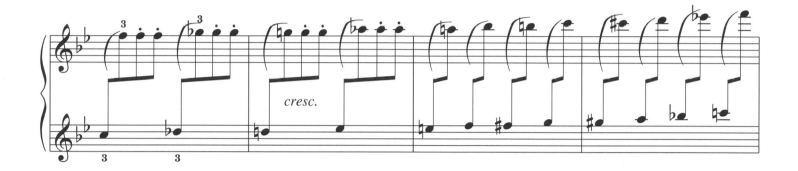

9

Begrüßung der Gäste
Welcoming the Guests

Allegro non troppo ♩ = 100 - 108

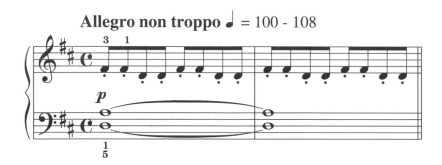

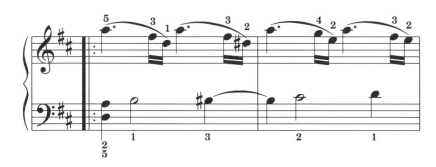

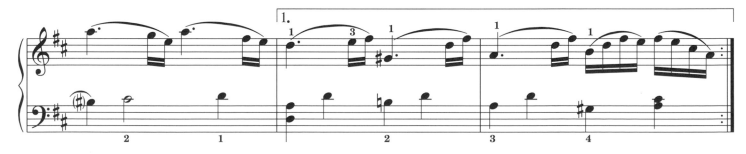

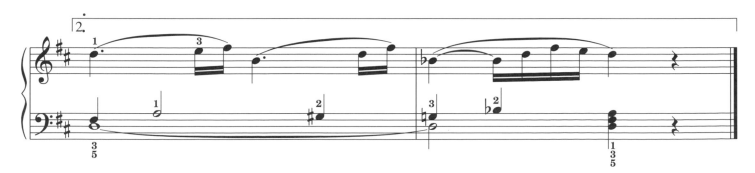

Marsch
March

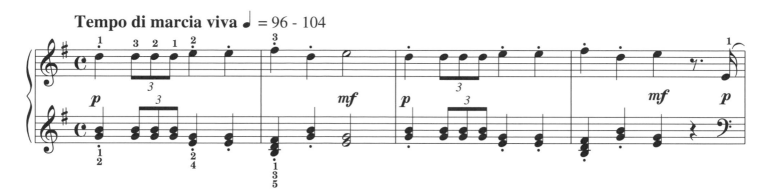

Onkel Drosselmeyer
Uncle Drosselmeyer

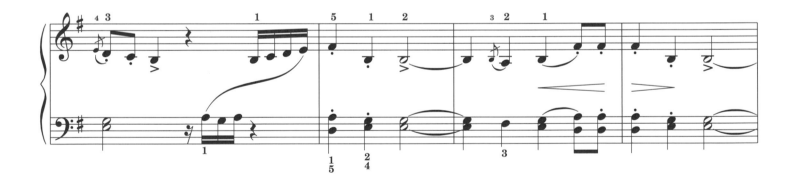

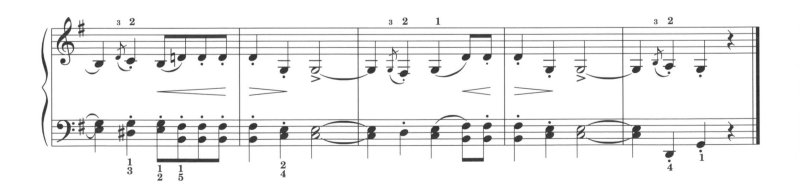

Klara und der Nussknacker
Clara and the Nutcracker

Andantino ♩ = 144

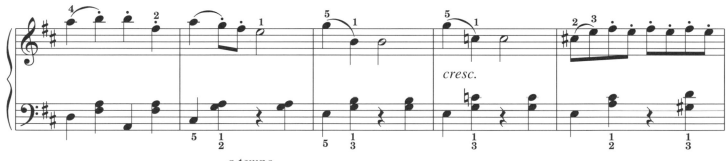

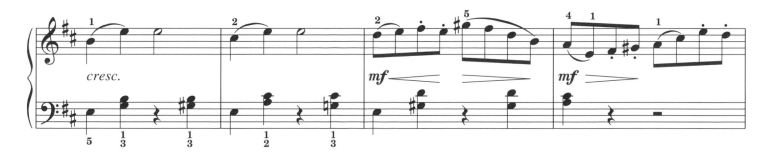

Più allegro ♩ = 168

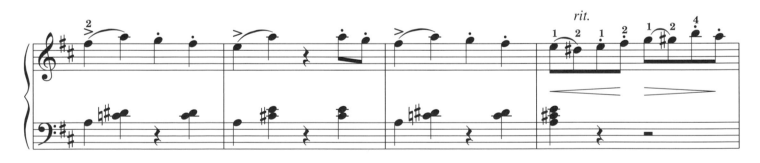

Tempo I

Più mosso

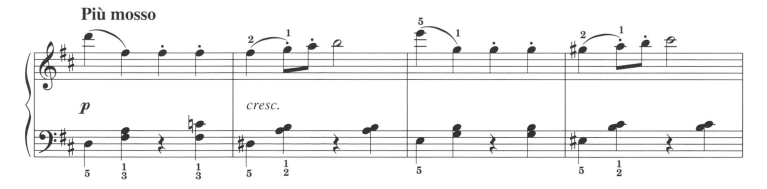

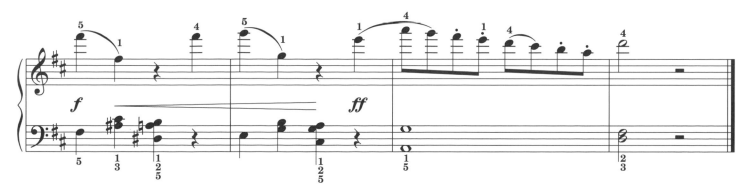

Großvatertanz
Grandfather's Dance

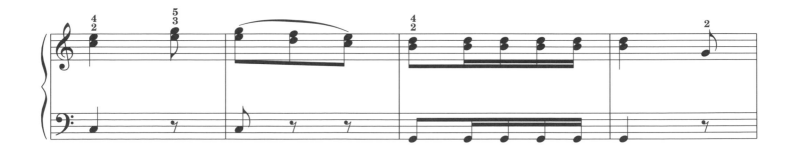

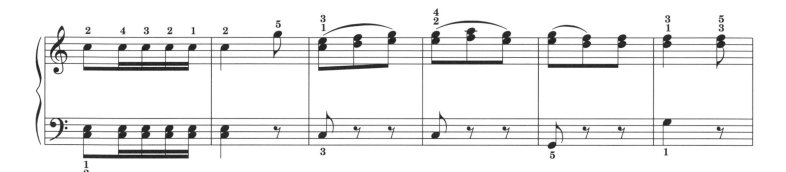

17

Pas de deux*

Klara und der Nussknacker-Prinz

Clara and the Nutcracker-Prince

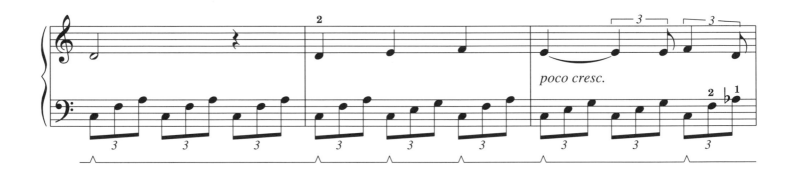

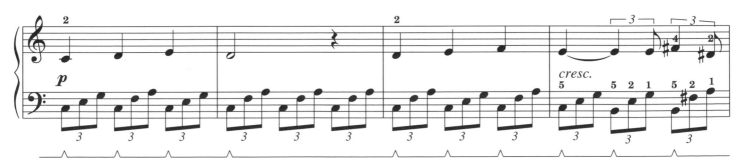

*Tanz zu zweit / Dance for two

Schneeflocken-Walzer
Snowflake Waltz

Tempo di Valse, ma con moto $\downarrow$. = 40 - 50

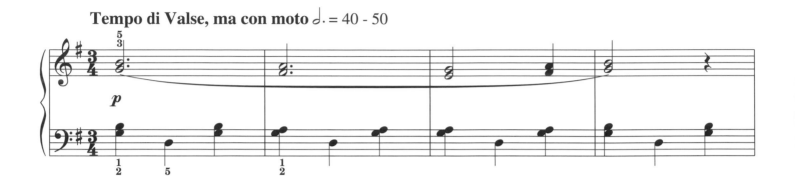

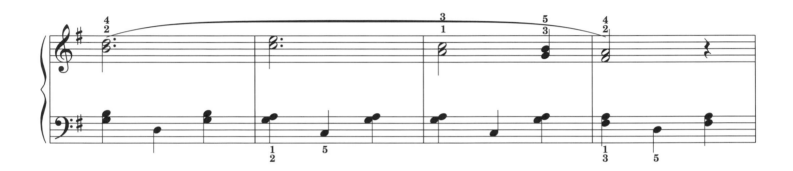

Spanischer Tanz
Spanish Dance

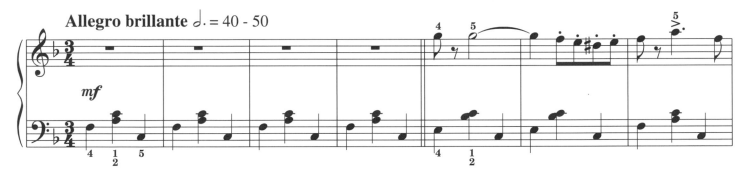

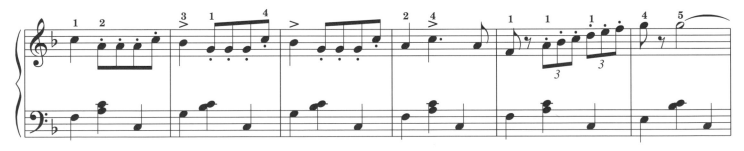

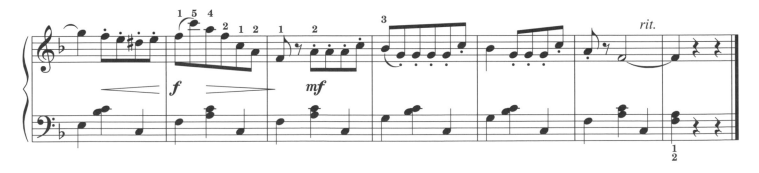

Arabischer Tanz
Arabian Dance

Allegro ♩ = 84 - 92

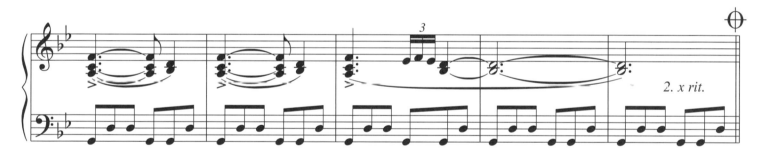

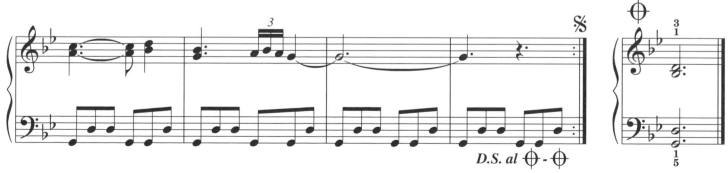

Chinesischer Tanz
Chinese Dance

Russischer Tanz
Russian Dance
(Trepak)

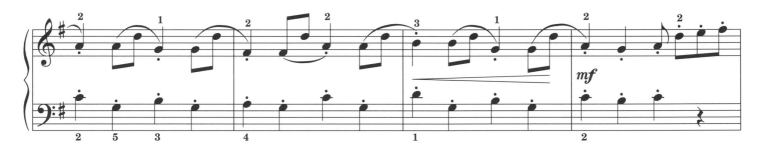

Tanz der Rohrflöten
Dance of the Reed Pipes

Mutter Gigogne
Mother Gigogne

Allegro giocoso ♩ = 100 - 108

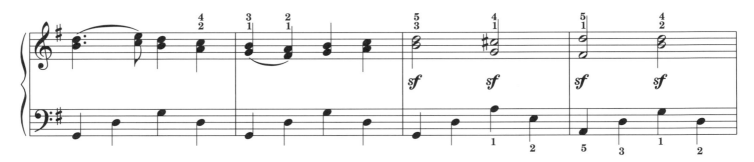

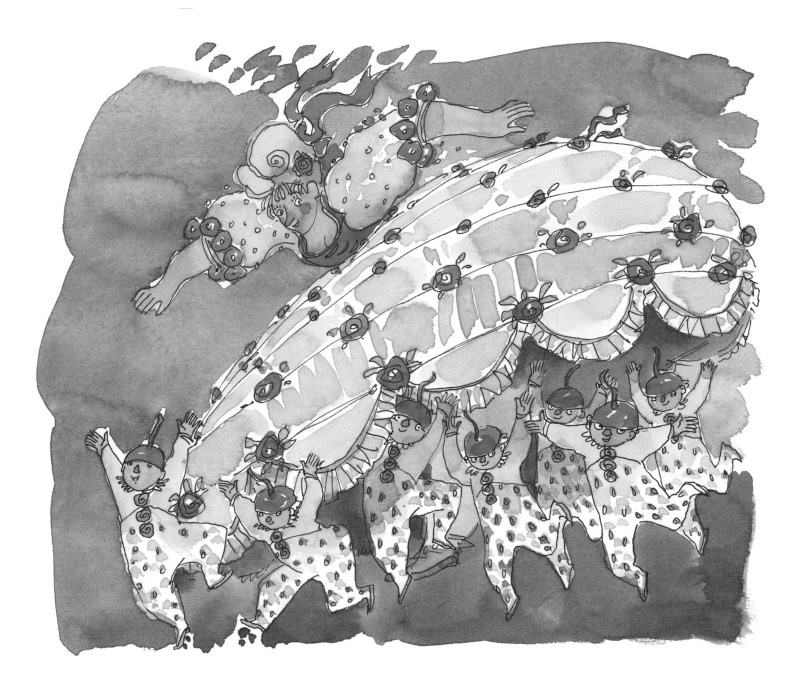

D.S. al Fine

Blumenwalzer
Waltz of the Flowers

Tempo di Valse ♩. = 50

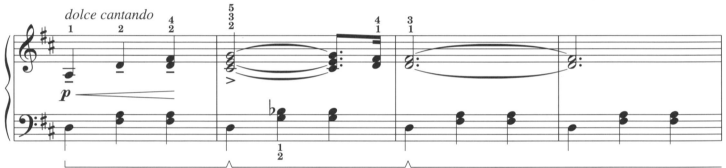

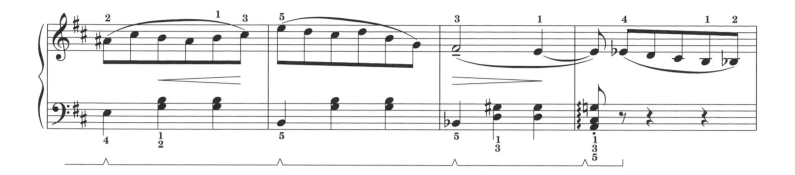

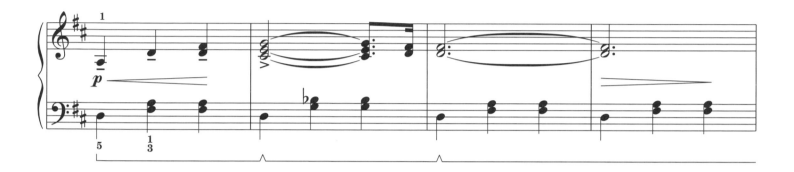

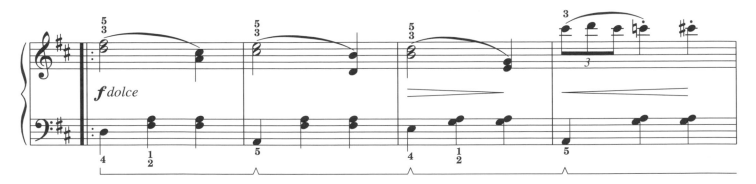

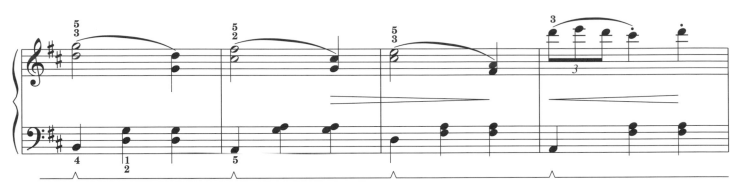

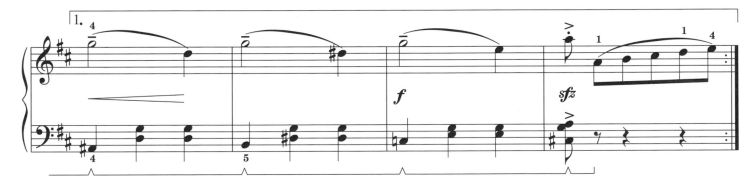

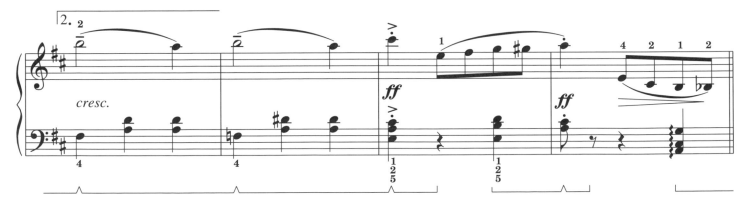

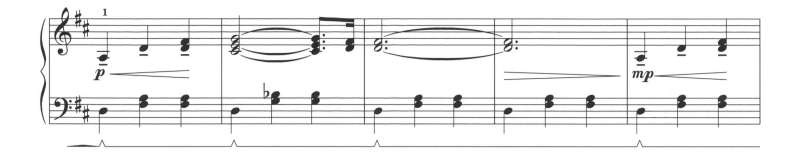

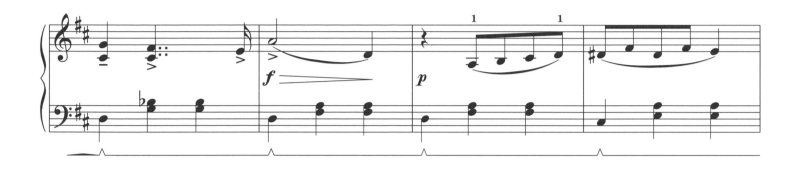

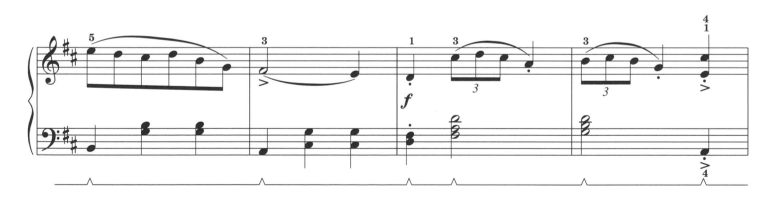

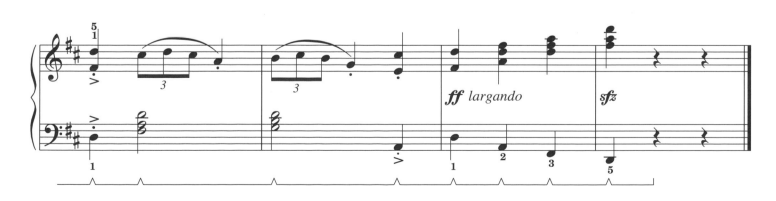

Finale (Walzer)
Finale (Waltz)

Tempo di Valse ♩. = 50

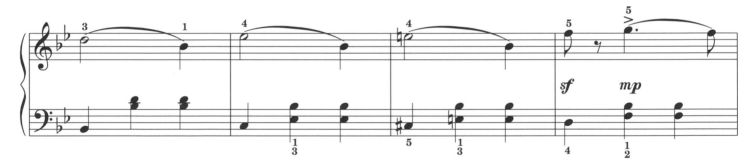

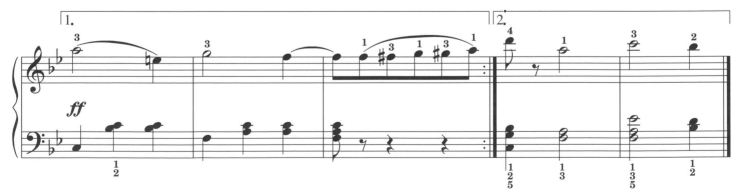

Schott Music, Mainz 60 113

Fantasievolle Klaviermusik / Imaginative Piano Music

Themenhefte in der Reihe „Schott Piano Classics"
Collections on various topics in the 'Schott Piano Classics' series
Herausgegeben von / Edited by Monika Twelsiek

- Unbekanntes entdecken
- Bekanntes in neuem Licht sehen
- Spannende und vielfarbige Themenhefte
- für den anspruchsvollen Unterricht
- leicht bis mittelschwer

- discover unfamiliar pieces
- see familiar pieces in a new light
- stimulating and colourful thematic collections
- for interesting and challenging tuition
- easy to intermediate level

Impressionismus / Impressionism

27 Originalwerke rund um Debussy – zum Eintauchen in die schwerelose Welt des Impressionismus

27 original pieces, grouped around Debussy – for immersion in the weightless world of impressionism
ED 9042

Programmmusik / Programme Music

40 Originalwerke, die mit programmatischen Titeln die Fantasie anregen – „Im Wald", „Regen", „Mondschein", „Sport", „Technik" u.a.

40 original pieces with programmatic titles stimulating the imagination – 'In the Forest', 'Rain', 'Moonlight', 'Sport', 'Technology' etc.
ED 9043

Reisebilder / Travel Pictures

37 Originalwerke zum Erkunden fremder Welten, – musikalische Ansichtskarten einer Reise in die unterschiedlichsten Länder

37 original pieces exploring foreign lands – musical postcards illustrate a journey in the most various countries
ED 9044

Emotionen / Emotions

35 Originalwerke zum Lachen und Weinen – schillernde Gefühle, die durch Musik erweckt und dargestellt werden

35 original pieces to inspire laughter and tears – dazzling feelings that are described and evoked by music
ED 9045

Walzer / Waltzes

48 Originalwerke von Mozart bis Ligeti – Walzer für jeden Tag: derb und übermütig, verträumt und melancholisch, langsam und virtuos

48 original pieces ranging from Mozart to Ligeti – waltzes for every day of the week: robust and exuberant, dreamy and melancholy, slow and elaborate
ED 9047

Nacht und Träume / Night and Dreams

36 Originalwerke zum Chillen, Relaxen, Entspannen – zum Eintauchen in die „Blaue Stunde", zum Tag- und Nacht-Träumen

36 original pieces for chilling out, relaxing, unwinding – for dipping into the twilight mood of dreams and daydreams
ED 9048

Tempo! Tempo!

40 schnelle und wilde, furiose und virtuose, rasante und riskante, billante und fulminante Originalwerke von Barock bis Rock – ein Etüdenheft der besonderen Art!

40 fast and furious, rousing and masterly, dazzling and brilliant original pieces ranging from Baroque to Rock, in a highly unusual book of studies!
ED 9049

Spielsachen / Toys

44 leichte Originalwerke für Kinder und Erwachsene – von Puppen, Teddybären, Spieluhren und Computerspielen zum Spielen und Erinnern

44 easy original pieces for children and adults to play, bringing back memories of dolls, teddy bears, musical boxes and computer games
ED 9055

Wasser / Water

25 Originalwerke zum Eintauchen in Quellen, Bäche, Flüsse, Meere – Wasser hat einen Klang und einen Rhythmus, es fließt – wie die Musik

25 original pieces plunge into springs, streams, rivers and seas – water has a sound and a rhythm, it flows – like music
ED 22276

Präludien / Preludes

40 Originalwerke aus fünf Jahrhunderten von Johann Sebastian Bach bis Nikolai Kapustin – eine klingende Geschichte der Gattung "Präludium"

40 original works ranging across five Centuries, from Johann Sebastian Bach to Nikolai Kapustin – a musical history of the Prelude
ED 23405

SCHOTT
www.schott-music.com

Piano Classic 3/2022